Anatomy of a Fleeting Muse

Kashika Chopra

BookLeaf Publishing

India | USA | UK

Dedication

To the Dead Poets who came before me. Thank you for making me believe I'm worthy.

To the daydreamers, thought daughters, girls who settle for nothing less than what they deserve.

To the brightest star in the sky, I dedicate these poems to you..

Acknowledgement

This short poetry book is the culmination of countless moments of inspiration, struggle, and growth.

To all the muses of my life—people(you know who you are), places, emotions, and the power of words—thank you for giving me endless reasons to write.

And, to all the girls fighting tooth and nail to be themselves.

I'm here for you.

Preface

When I was 13, I read a book that was more than just a story—it was a mirror, a puzzle, and a revelation. At first, it hurt me deeply, as though it was reaching into my soul and reshaping everything I thought I knew. To grasp its meaning was to wrestle with the very essence of my existence.

But over time, the book and I became inseparable. It seeped into my thoughts, my emotions, and my being. It became me, and I became it.

Within its pages was a poem that has lingered with me ever since:
"Through all of youth, I was looking for you, without knowing what I was looking for."

Those words encapsulated everything I had ever felt but couldn't articulate—not accomplishment, not pride, but the profound sense of being whole.

And now, this collection is my completion. These poems are my reflections, my search, and my answers. I hope, in some way, they become yours too.

The discovery in losing yourself

There is youth in beauty,
A sly, conniving thing that slips into the
periphery,
The edge of the world you grab onto,
with the perfect calluses that tell a million
somethings,
the story that was you.
The story carved into the scars on your hands,
the freckles no insecurity could hide,
the slight crook of your nose when you faced
convictions
that latched onto you--only to leave you
rugged, breathless, beaten and broken inside.
With the hazy lens through which you view
the world,
in your star-dazed eyes and wounds you saw
in the night sky,
you dragged it out of the sky you called the
ocean,
the tainted body,

the worshipper of slights and faulty doors,
the broken nails and jagged cores,
of that heart, you deemed so pure.
Nobody was ever yours,
but you, even though the soap couldn't melt
away your sins,
even though every hand that touched your
heart was never yours,
the chipped nails and teeth,
with which you fought,
and a million times, you lost.
You lost,
Time and Time again.
You lost to your misery,
you lost to your demons,
but you could never lose yourself.
You could never lose that ugly birthmark your
friends made fun of,
you could never lose the way you laughed,
you could never lose that time you called your
youth,
nor the way your mind was an overwhelming
ocean.
The way you mastered the art of deception,
the art of mascara that ran down your scars,

the ringing of bells you called love, but really
was infidelity,
how you survived on the rot of the loveless
and the unholy.
No, you could never lose yourself.

But you could never win, either.

Sugar and Spice

I keep seeing my eyes every day, wandering
down the hallways at night, in my dreams, the
way I see the calluses on my hands.
I have eyes, I realised when I was three, a nose
when I was four, hands to roll dough, and
knees to play in the mud.
I had dewdrops collected on my forehead,
crowns of grass blades, and the flintstones I
cast into the fire that made it my childhood.
But could fulfilment be as easily filled as loss?
Could I empty the boxes of my childhood in
one go?
And let go of the razor blades still hung in the
corner of my mind, beckoning to slit my life
open like the pages of a book?
Could I as easily forgive my body as I had
when I was a child?
"sugar, spice and everything nice"?

Girlhood

is a tangle of earphones on the metro
when you have 30 minutes to spare and
too many thoughts, three different lip glosses
on your desk because you can't tell when one
has
reached the bottom, and you can't be
bothered
to check, no clothes to wear, even with a
wardrobe
 full because you buy pieces separately
and you can't even find their pair, just like
you're
struggling to see how you could ever find your
own match, but it's okay
 because girlhood is coffee
shop tea and being kicked out of restaurants
for staying too long all because you kept on
talking
more than you could afford to eat with other
girls

that sparkle and shimmer and cannot see
their worth
like you cannot see your own.

Summer

The smell of fresh chlorophyll in the air and
the sweat of leaves as they await their
persecution
from the sun. And in my memories, it thrives,
the sweet, rash sound the motor makes across
the lawn as the fresh dew plunges to freedom
and
on my cheek await the lies I told myself like a
consolation prize to a weeping child,
not knowing how they would evaporate
and leave me with nothing but the dust of
memories of last summer.
When our ice-creams melt, a weeping child.
And our tongues turn every shade of
childhood before
they start churning out knives, stabbing in
the back.
Before the tattoo on your wrist, you hide from
everybody else
before the oath that spilt your blood like
wine.

And where were we?
We were bunny-hopping across the lawn,
the smell of maple syrup in our noses as we
panted and ran
a million miles from our lives, discovering
how long could we last until we were bloody
and broken inside?
But this was summer,
the year, I lied to myself and laughed at the
truths,
the memories that haunt me now, like
Catherine did to Heathcliff, and by the moors
the sun watches over us like frail children.
But we clung to our lives, unaware
we could throw it away like parachutes to fly.

We must kill something to begin again

There is rain in my heart,
Full of quaint fears and hopeful tears.
Rain on the roof, at the edge of my brain,
transmigration of the leaves as they turn
copper and grey.
There is death under my feet and blood on my
hands,
I killed the memory once, twice would be in
agonising rage.
To see the earth blush pink and the blank
page in its glory, arid.
To set my soul to stone and the summer's fate
to weary rain.
I must await autumn
and set the world's stage again
to begin life's act until it all turns into a
euphoric campaign;
we must kill something to begin again.

Sum of the Universe

You are the sum of every person you have ever met.

You are the flowers your roommate buys in the morning.

You are the songs the old lady listens to on the subway to buy groceries.

You are every thought you read, every musing possessing your mind like the wind sweeping through an orchid.

You are the citrus perfume your mother wears every morning and the crinkling of her eyes when she laughs.

You are your friend's mascara, which she's been using since she was 15, and the pasta recipe you saw on YouTube a few years back. Even if people don't stay with you, their memories and habits always do. And it moulds you into the person you are today.

Palimpsest: An Ode to Revenge

I always thought there were ways of being and then not being. To erase your pasts and lives from the piece of paper we call destiny. Or the soil that lives- over and over again, replenishes its mortality until those living beneath start their peaceful existence again. They have scraped off our voices from history, like debris from the official record- written and expunged have our names been. If you dwell deeper into the rough drafts of the original story, you will find our words. The scars and the wrinkles on the elders' foreheads trace the map of a world that once had been overwritten by many and erased by none. With the victory that came upon the destruction of the statue at the town square that afternoon came the bitter aftertaste of the present: *what now?* For all that is bright, precious, and bejewelled comes the

vulnerability of the broken, the fragility of a
wounded soldier. And to start over again.
From the minds of our ancestors–my
ancestors and their tainted lineage have their
fettered dreams come to me like smoke
swirling from a caged room.
They told us, "You can never escape your
family's grasp around the throat of the
present".
It is in the banyan they planted, withered
with old age, omniscient to the blood that
nourished its sadistic roots while it stood
unmoving to the tyranny against our own. It
is the only thing that has not altered in our
modern world. But to revise our past means
starting over. To not speak the language
guzzling out of our tongues like knives, to not
cook *biryani* for dinner. And our love songs to
the past would be love songs heard in the
background of waltzes.
To reveal something is the art of the
storyteller, and with the fragile wounds, you
rubbed salt over the merciless cages on our
lips while you rewrote our pasts and took
what was ours. It may not be easy to forget

that hatred for it has been passed down to us
like blood-sworn oaths we take.
We will take our revenge.

Rue

Rue, rue galore
Rue in the streets flooding with tears,
In the walking of the man holding the
flowers,
For his lover, as his tears water the withered
flowers
Rue in the girl as she holds the books she calls
her true love.
The pages were stained and blackened with a
glimpse of remorse.
Rue in the way you hold me in your wallet,
holding someone else's hand,
Loving, ever-loving heart of mine, you kept it
in your pocket,
ready to be discarded at the nearest doorstep,
bundled with blankets and cold that could
never be erased as you threw me out of your
blazing home, bleeding with love for someone
else.

Rue, as the first pair of shoes I bought,
stepped out into the ruthless streets of New
York.
Rue, as my eyes blurred every night, looking
for words I may never find.
My head, a dull, throbbing menace dancing
with my heart,
gazing out from the eyes of a lonely girl in a
lonely city.
Rue, as I stared at her, there was nothing I
could do
to save her from herself.
Leaping out of the balcony, a leap of faith,
a leap of trust, with no one to catch her but
the bare icy ground thirsty for the colour of
rose on its stones.
And heart bleeding on its skin.
Rue, as the last tear drop fell from her eyes,
Drop
Drop
End of the new generation.

Ruined

It is strange to be alive in a broken, bloodied
world,
To have the courage to face the same things
over and over again,
but do not crawl inside your body and hope
someone breaks the silence and reveals what
terrible people we all are.
But still,
love is an undressing,
and in hushed tones,
loves you for your most ruined self.

Fourth Wave

Those rules, those lines and curves that you
bind us to,
remember, we are more than that,
we are more than objects for men to woo
and art to be perfected and graded.
We are minds and souls and hearts
sewn into one,
we are voices and colours and hands
lighting candles of incandescence,
illuminating the minds and souls of those
indefatigable in their efforts to fight--
fight for who they are, as their blood boils in
rage
but wear masks of poise and grace.
Even as we toil and labour under the wrathful
gazes of those who condemn us,
we see a future,
a future, a sea we must cross to enjoy the sun
over the horizon,
our pride gleamed as bright as the light

that surges through our veins, light and
synergy,
lightning at our fingertips that burns those
who stake us, blaze us alive,
those ashes you pick up are not our hope yet,
but skins we shed as we hurdle on,
sweat and blood and bones of our ancestry
mixed with aplomb and....
fazed, are you with us?
For we are more than just pretty faces and
murmurs
or the turtles this world stands upon,
we are women.

The world is ending, and I'm wondering what to eat for dinner

The world is a scrap iron, and they are its
miners,
digging coal, digging blood, digging the word
mercy out of the home shed of the crestfallen,
and
we are at its painful mercy.
It digs and digs until the word mercy turns
into bloodshed,
and it digs and digs and digs our eyes out of
their sockets,
another one in the Museum of Genocide.
There is blood seeping into the sap of trees,
quivering branches bloodthirsty, entrapping
hands, legs, melodies of the forgotten,
and our voices are nothing but waltzes to
dance to, mouth an arrow aiming at your
heart, but stop.
Don't shed a tear, for your eyes are all but
foreign to you now,

look through the negatives of your x-ray film,
and you will only see their pleas staring at you
in the face,
but you will be blind anyway.
They could be your children, mothers, fathers,
sisters, or brothers.
Press a button, call a friend, and use your eyes
for help.
Because we have eyes, and ears, and hearts,
we are sinews and joints and blood that run
deeper and deeper than your sins.
Remember, this scrap iron has a memory
forged into its bleeding heart.
And it's called karma.

Our Story

Home is the place where we come to after
each struggling day,
home is the place where the hearth thrives,
and the fire turns friendly,
where chairs, shelves, and tables are scooped
out, an offering for each smile,
home is where the smell of roast chicken and
parmesan thrives,
Home tells our own story.
It is the musing of our beating hearts,
our dreams come to life,
embellish it, paint it, mould it from shattered
pieces,
even if it's just walls and paint, the
camouflaged writings tell my story.
Home is the ubiquitous silence that comes to
mind after each jaded day,
home is the top of the mountain, the
adrenaline-pumping fillip,
home is reading books as the raindrops patter
on your window like a foreign guest.

Even when we strip it bare and tear it down,
home is where I choose to be.
Home is the screams and fights and sorrows
swivelled into cordiality,
home is the storm with an evil eye, the smell
of burnt food,
the failures as the current washes away to the
shore,
home is listening to music as the hurricane
dissipates into oblivion.
Home is the place at the end of our story.

NightShade

I write to make dreams real.
Feral claws, ridges and nooks
gnawing at the peripheries of my vision.
Together, we are snow-capped mountains and
valleys that poison my water.
Nightshade, sparkle, 3:00 am
And you are companions with my thoughts.
We could be more than this--
We could be legions that await their mortal
purgatory.
We could be paint swirls in the mundane
water I use to paint your eyes.
Blood sworn oaths, fear in your iris, the passage of
time
Is this all we could be?
Transcend into the delusions you call history,
and I'll give you another one to make.

A-Lived

To have lived and been alive,
are two separate things,
for it means standing at the edge of a cliff,
and tasting true ichor on your tongue.
To have lived, you have to be seen,
to be alive, you have seen.

"You are the knife I turn inside myself"

I wish the world were ending tomorrow.
Then I could take the next train, arrive at
your doorstep in Vienna and say, "I was never
much of a romantic, but the bumblebee
aerodynamically shouldn't be able to fly. But
it doesn't know that.
It goes on flying anyways."
We stare at our wounds instead. And watch a
thousand sunsets before the world ends. In
the twilight, ask me again.
I waited so long for youth without knowing I
was staring at it the entire time. It is a kind of
love, isn't it?
Should we fill our diaries with thoughts that
have become all but corporate memories?
Can we forget all about our "cool lives"?
and I will not mention how your hair feels in
my hands,
my mouth an infinite distance from you that
we forget the Sun is nearer to our destiny
than our own fates.

As if we weren't certain.
As if it wasn't my confession.

Pretty Things with their Knives of Poison

There are coloured stains in my tea,
and I wonder how many times I should die to
be that blue stain in my blue pea tea.
Flowers that drowned and pyres of my past
laid down, **bare black**
—the tainted lineage of my ancestors.
I read Russian poetry, but all I can think of is
blue pea tea.
Pain in the void of my tar black soul; cigarette
smoke coating the poison I drink.
Withered flowers, dull moonstone, painting my
bannisters blue,
for it is the colour of poison lathering the
sliced blade like an eager guest.
Each day passes, and the tea paints itself blue,
a blank canvas filled with the eulogies and
promises we never fulfilled.
It's Alice Blue, the poison that keeps me alive,
a painting of ponds and gods that play in the
garden full of dreams.

Sunken eyebags for my sunken hopes, but
look at them—
Pretty things with their knives of poison.

A Love Story in 1946

I can build a page for you out of the broken
silences in this world.
I can carve up houses, bones, laughter, and
love–I know you never had.
I can conjure rain with pretty little droplets
over pretty white porches.
But amidst the plentiful branches and the
caging sky, the sun will still scorch.
And green branches still plenty under the
spell of a morning sky
because you were an abyss and it was a jailer.
Marking you, like a broken clock, over and
over again.
I waited for you till the ink spilled out of my
lungs
but I know the hallowed beatings of my heart
mean you'll never come home.
And I know the tears falling,
the oblivion in the letters I wrote every
morning,
crushed and littered,

flooding the basement and my heart with
words I know I will never send.
But I spell out her name on the dying trees
anyway,
Home, home, home.
Maybe we'll just have a few more seconds,
a few more goodbyes
but it looks like smoke is pouring out of your
garage like failed arson, and there is no room
for me.
Maybe you'll never come home.
Maybe the axe I plunge into the darkness will
kill me anyway.
Maybe I crashed my car and built my home,
alone, alone, alone.
And the gunshots I hear every morning from
the birds are just holes in my chest,
and the poem I write is an aubade for my life.
Maybe I could never be the lighthouse, but
you were just a shipwreck,
Undiscovered, undisclosed, unexplored.

Musing #2

I hope at some point in your life, you'll realise achieving perfection will never be enough.

There will always be that one thing you want, that one person you crave to be. I hope you empathise with the child who craved love in their soul's broken parts, waiting for wildflowers to bloom from its pieces. I hope you thank yourself daily for showing up, for fighting when no one is fighting for you except you, for waking up each morning and telling yourself, "I'm alive, I'm alive, I'm alive". Just know that every molecule of oxygen that keeps your blood red sparks magic that works against the odds to keep you alive because you are the Chosen One. Your mind, heart, and soul fought the earth and stars to be here. You have created art in places you didn't even know existed but beat for you, only you.

Lady Lazarus

Tonight, that idyllic laughter feels like rain
that cowers over my shoulder,
hell-bent on breaking me down.
But I'm not mad at you for winning, emperors
past, with your haunting history,
destroying something that can't be rebuilt.
I've lain bricks by bricks, hammered my truth
and dug into the grave I call ancient history,
but it haunts me as Catherine did to
Heathcliff.
Bruised legs, bruised cheeks, demons lurking
by,
But beware, I ate an apple from the Garden of
Eden,
and was born of the light that casts diamonds
out of thin air,
and shaping my teeth into daggers.
But I cannot stop the darkness shadowed by
the light.

Maybe the chants and the letters I write to
you every morning could find a way to reach
you again,
inflexions that feel like shards as we bake an
apple pie together from the apples we picked
together.
Flick your wrists, and you might see me again.

Musing #3

Would it be easier to fill the air in the balloon I call my lungs and float in a never-found eternity?

If this is how life was, was it just? Floating, existing, a plane created just for our thoughts to exist—to live and live and die with a coffin of moments, a coffin of how we discovered the secret of life buried just with us—our secret key to unlock the secrets of the universe?

We live in our minds sometimes, a watercolour array of thoughts and a feature film that's never to hit the theatres because we're just too busy holding memories rather than making them. After all, we're just made to live, to dream because sometimes that's just more real than the world reflected in our eyes. If our eyes were just a projection of the things we were blinded to, would we still wait for moments to happen to us? Or would we make a scrapbook glued together by every tear, fear, and joyous memory we've ever had? Maybe we're just existing for ourselves, or maybe we would finally get time to exist when we're dead.

YOUth

"Look at you. You're young. And you're scared.
Why are you so scared?
Stop being paralysed. Stop swallowing your
words. Stop caring what others think.
Wear what you want. Say what you want.
Listen to the music you want to listen to. Play
it loud as hell and dance to it.
Go for a drive at midnight and forget you
have school the next day.
Stop waiting for Friday. Live. Live right now.
Do it NOW. Take risks. Tell secrets. This life is
yours.
When will you realise that you can do
whatever you want?"

In my Head, I do Everything Right

I am the biggest paradox I've ever known. I'm insecure in everything I do, yet I love myself to the point of total narcissism.
Warm and endearing one second and aloof the next. Some days, we could talk about the Universe until sunrise; others, a simple smile in my direction is too much to expect.
I have a roof over my head and food on the table. No limitations. There are no walls I need to break down. But I'm not a genius. Not a superstar, not this incredible human being. And my greatest fear is that I will never do anything.
People with incredible backstories change the world.
Can I?